MoD by Google
The Latest Innovation Shaping the World of Tomorrow

A New AI That's Outpacing Human Intelligence and Transforming Industries

Modesta E. Jackson

Table of Contents

Introduction

The world has entered an era where artificial intelligence is no longer just a futuristic concept but a present reality reshaping industries at an astonishing pace. From healthcare to finance, entertainment to scientific research, AI has become the silent force driving efficiency, innovation, and problem-solving on an unprecedented scale. What was once limited to experimental labs and theoretical discussions has now evolved into systems capable of generating human-like text, creating ultra-realistic videos, and even assisting in scientific discoveries that would have taken human researchers decades to unravel.

Among the tech giants pushing the boundaries of AI, Google stands at the forefront. With its deep investments in machine learning and artificial intelligence research, the company has consistently introduced groundbreaking innovations that redefine the way machines think and process information. From the early days of search engine algorithms to the development of DeepMind, Google has made AI smarter, faster, and more capable. Now, a new breakthrough is set to change everything: Mixture of Depths, or MoD.

At its core, MoD is an evolution of the transformer model, a technology that powers most modern AI applications, including language models and large-scale data processing. The challenge with traditional transformers is that they allocate the same amount of computational power to every piece of information they process, whether it is essential or not. This inefficiency has long been a bottleneck in AI performance, forcing models to expend unnecessary resources on trivial data points. MoD changes that by allowing the AI to selectively focus its processing power on the most critical parts of a sequence while skipping over less significant details. The result is an AI that is not only faster but also more efficient, capable of producing better results while using fewer resources.

The implications of this technology are vast. Imagine reading a book where your mind instinctively skips over the filler words and focuses only on the most important parts, allowing you to absorb information at twice the speed without losing comprehension. This is essentially how MoD works, making AI smarter in how it processes language and data. This efficiency could mean massive improvements in AI-generated content, real-time communication, and even how AI-powered assistants interact with users. It opens the door to models that require less computational power yet perform at levels that surpass anything we've seen before.

The purpose of this book is to break down these complex innovations in a way that is accessible to everyone. AI advancements often sound technical and overwhelming, but their impact on the world is something that affects us all. Whether it's through smarter chatbots, more lifelike video generation, or AI-powered scientific research, the changes unfolding right now are shaping the future in ways that many people have yet to fully grasp. By understanding Google's latest contributions to AI, we gain insight into where technology is headed and how it will shape the industries and daily lives of the future.

This book will take a deep dive into Google's latest AI breakthroughs, explaining how MoD is revolutionizing machine intelligence, how AI-generated video is becoming more realistic and accessible, and how Google's AI-powered research tools are solving decade-long scientific mysteries in mere days. Along the way, we'll uncover the mechanics behind these innovations and explore the profound ways they are set to transform the world.

Artificial intelligence is no longer a distant possibility—it is here, evolving at an extraordinary speed. And as Google leads the charge, the question is no longer whether AI will change the future, but rather, how quickly it will reshape everything we know.

Chapter 1: The Evolution of AI and Google's Role

Artificial intelligence has come a long way from its early days, evolving from simple rule-based systems to complex neural networks capable of mimicking human-like reasoning. The journey began with early AI models in the mid-20th century, where researchers attempted to build machines that could process information and make logical decisions. These early efforts were largely symbolic AI, relying on predefined rules and logic to solve problems. However, the limitations of these systems became apparent—they struggled to handle real-world uncertainty and lacked the ability to learn from experience.

The next major breakthrough came with the development of artificial neural networks, which attempted to mimic the structure of the human brain by using interconnected nodes to process information. Initially, these models were relatively simple and faced limitations due to computational power constraints. But as technology advanced, so did AI, leading to the rise of machine learning, where models could be trained on vast datasets and improve over time.

Deep learning, a more sophisticated form of neural networks, revolutionized AI by allowing models to process information in multiple layers, extracting complex patterns from raw data. This led to significant advancements in computer vision, natural language processing, and autonomous decision-making. AI was no longer just a set of predefined rules—it became capable of recognizing speech, translating languages, and even generating human-like text.

One of the key players in this AI revolution has been Google, particularly through its DeepMind division. Founded with the vision of building AI systems that can think and learn like humans, DeepMind has consistently pushed the boundaries of what is possible. One of its early breakthroughs was AlphaGo, an AI that defeated human world champions in the complex board game Go, demonstrating an ability to strategize at a superhuman level. This was a pivotal moment in AI history, proving that machine intelligence could surpass human intuition in fields once thought to be exclusive to human cognition.

DeepMind didn't stop there. It went on to develop AlphaFold, an AI model that solved one of biology's greatest mysteries—predicting the 3D structure of proteins with remarkable accuracy. This achievement had profound implications for medicine, allowing researchers to accelerate drug discovery and understand diseases at a molecular level. Meanwhile, Google continued to integrate AI into its core products, enhancing search algorithms, optimizing translations, and even developing AI-powered writing and creative tools.

As AI continued to evolve, the challenge shifted from simply making models more powerful to making them more efficient. Traditional deep learning models required enormous computational resources, making them expensive to run and limiting their scalability. This is where Google's latest innovation, Mixture of Depths (MoD), comes in. By rethinking how AI processes information, Google has found a way to optimize computational efficiency without sacrificing performance, marking yet another leap forward in AI technology.

From simple neural networks to deep learning and now to efficiency-focused AI models like MoD, the trajectory of artificial intelligence has been one of constant evolution. And with each breakthrough, AI is becoming more embedded in our daily lives, shaping everything from healthcare to entertainment and beyond. Google's role in this transformation has been undeniable, consistently pushing AI beyond its limits and bringing the future closer with every new development.

Artificial intelligence has undergone a radical transformation over the past decade, with the introduction of transformer-based models marking one of the most significant breakthroughs in machine learning. These models revolutionized natural language processing, enabling AI to understand and generate human-like text, translate languages with near-human fluency, and even engage in complex reasoning. Transformers became the backbone of AI-driven systems, powering everything from chatbots to content recommendation engines. However, as powerful as they are, they also come with inherent limitations that have created bottlenecks in efficiency, cost, and scalability.

Traditional transformers operate on a simple principle: they process every word (or token) in a sequence with the same level of computational effort. Whether a word carries crucial meaning or is just filler, the model dedicates equal attention to it, leading to excessive and often unnecessary computations. This brute-force approach, while effective, has made large-scale AI models incredibly resource-intensive, requiring massive amounts of hardware and energy to function. Training these models can take weeks or even months, consuming computational resources at a scale that is both expensive and environmentally unsustainable.

As AI adoption grew, so did the demand for more efficient architectures that could deliver the same, if not better, results with fewer resources. The challenge was clear: AI needed a way to allocate its computational power more strategically, focusing only on the most relevant parts of a sequence while skipping over less important details. This is where Mixture of Depths (MoD) introduces a game-changing innovation.

MoD reimagines how transformers process information by introducing a more dynamic approach to computation. Instead of treating every token equally, MoD selectively routes only the most significant tokens through the intensive self-attention and multi-layered processing pipelines, while allowing less important ones to bypass certain computations. This selective processing means the model can perform just as well—sometimes even better—while using a fraction of the computational resources.

To visualize this, imagine reading a dense textbook. If you were to read every word with equal concentration, it would take a long time to get through, even if many sentences were repetitive or contained background information you already understood. However, if you could instinctively recognize the most important parts and focus your attention only on those, skipping over what you don't need, you would absorb the key information much faster without losing comprehension. This is exactly how MoD optimizes AI processing.

One of the biggest advantages of this new approach is that it significantly reduces the computational burden without compromising accuracy. In fact, research has shown that MoD models can sometimes outperform traditional transformers despite using fewer resources. By allocating compute power more effectively, these models can scale larger, train faster, and run on lower hardware requirements, making them more accessible and cost-effective.

The shift from traditional transformers to more efficient architectures like MoD marks an important milestone in AI development. It signals a new phase where intelligence is not just about power but also about precision—doing more with less. This innovation is set to reshape the AI landscape, making machine learning more scalable, sustainable, and widely applicable across different industries. As MoD continues to evolve, it holds the potential to unlock even greater advancements, pushing AI beyond its current limits and into a future where speed, efficiency, and intelligence go hand in hand.

Chapter 2: Understanding Mixture of Depths (MoD)

Mixture of Depths (MoD) represents a new leap in artificial intelligence, refining how AI models process information with greater efficiency. At its core, MoD is an advanced variation of the transformer architecture, designed to solve one of the most pressing issues in AI—computational inefficiency. While traditional transformers revolutionized machine learning with their ability to handle vast amounts of data, they did so with an inherent flaw: they allocated the same level of processing power to every token in a sequence, regardless of its importance. This approach led to unnecessary computations, increasing costs, slowing down performance, and making AI models more resource-hungry than they needed to be.

MoD addresses this challenge by introducing a selective processing mechanism that allows the model to dynamically decide which tokens require deep computational attention and which can bypass certain layers without losing meaning. Instead of applying equal effort across all tokens, MoD intelligently routes only the most critical ones through the expensive self-attention and MLP (multi-layer perceptron) computations, while allowing the less significant ones to take a more efficient shortcut. This is achieved through a per-token router, a mechanism that assigns a priority score to each token in a sequence. The tokens with the highest scores go through the full depth of processing, while the lower-priority ones follow a more lightweight path.

To put this into perspective, imagine reading a news article. A traditional transformer would process every single word with the same intensity, whether it's an important noun that carries meaning or a common word like "the" or "and." MoD, on the other hand, functions more like a human reader skimming through a text—focusing on the meaningful words that shape the context while instinctively skipping over filler words without losing comprehension. This results in a smarter allocation of computing power, significantly reducing processing time while maintaining, or even improving, accuracy.

One of MoD's key advantages is that it operates within a static computation graph, meaning it doesn't introduce unpredictable behavior that would disrupt hardware efficiency. The model is designed to predefine the maximum number of tokens that receive full computation (for example, 12.5% of all tokens in a given sequence), ensuring that system resources are used optimally. This structure not only lowers computational overhead but also enables larger models to be trained on the same budget, pushing AI capabilities further without exponentially increasing costs.

The impact of MoD is profound. By reducing the number of FLOPs (floating point operations per second) required per forward pass, AI models become faster, leaner, and more scalable. They can be trained for longer durations without requiring excessive hardware, making AI research more sustainable and accessible. Moreover, because MoD improves efficiency without sacrificing performance, it enables higher-quality AI applications in real-world scenarios, from natural language processing to real-time decision-making in autonomous systems.

In essence, MoD represents a fundamental shift in AI architecture. Instead of simply making models bigger and more powerful, it introduces a strategic approach to computation, making AI systems work smarter, not harder. As AI continues to advance, MoD is paving the way for a future where intelligence is not only about raw computing power but about precision, efficiency, and adaptability—a crucial step toward making AI more practical, cost-effective, and widely usable across industries.

Artificial intelligence, at its core, is about recognizing patterns and making sense of data, but not all pieces of information hold equal value. Some words, phrases, or symbols in a dataset carry more meaning than others, just as in human conversation, where certain words drive the conversation forward while others merely connect thoughts. Traditional transformer models, however, have long been inefficient in handling this discrepancy—they process every token with the same level of computational effort, treating trivial words with the same intensity as key terms that define the meaning of a sentence. This approach, while powerful, results in wasted computation and limits scalability.

Mixture of Depths (MoD) introduces a new paradigm by implementing dynamic allocation of compute power, ensuring that only the most relevant tokens receive deep processing. Instead of blindly applying full computation to every token in a sequence, MoD's architecture learns to prioritize—identifying which tokens require intensive computation and which can safely bypass certain layers. This method significantly enhances performance, allowing AI to operate with higher efficiency and reduced computational costs.

The mechanism that makes this possible is known as per-token routing. Rather than applying uniform processing across an entire sequence, MoD employs a routing system that assigns a unique scalar weight to each token based on its relevance. These weights act as decision-making scores, determining whether a particular token will pass through the expensive self-attention and MLP layers or take a more computationally efficient shortcut. Tokens with high importance scores are fully processed, while those with lower scores are routed around certain computations, dramatically reducing the workload without sacrificing output quality.

To understand this in practical terms, imagine scanning through a research paper. When reading, your brain naturally focuses on the key concepts, absorbing critical information while skimming past redundant words. This is exactly how MoD optimizes AI performance—by ensuring that only the most valuable parts of a sequence receive full computational attention. This not only improves processing speed but also enables AI models to scale more effectively, allowing for more complex tasks to be handled within the same resource constraints.

Another advantage of MoD's routing system is that it operates within a static computational framework, meaning that despite its dynamic allocation of processing power, it maintains a structured approach that optimizes hardware utilization. Unlike some adaptive AI models that introduce unpredictability and disrupt parallel processing efficiency, MoD ensures that resources are used effectively by setting a predefined limit on the number of tokens receiving full computation. For example, if only 12.5% of tokens are allocated full processing power, the model ensures that system resources are dedicated to the most important data points, maximizing efficiency.

This breakthrough is not just about making AI faster—it's about making it smarter in resource distribution. By selectively routing computational effort to where it is truly needed, MoD reduces processing costs, improves response times, and enables AI to operate at a larger scale without requiring exponential increases in computing power. The result is an AI system that delivers equal or superior performance while consuming a fraction of the energy, making it a game-changer for real-world applications that demand both speed and precision.

As AI continues to evolve, the ability to intelligently allocate computing resources will become one of the defining factors of its success. MoD's per-token routing system represents a critical step in this direction, paving the way for AI models that are not just more powerful but also more efficient, adaptable, and sustainable.

Artificial intelligence has made remarkable progress in recent years, largely due to the widespread adoption of transformer models. These models revolutionized natural language processing, enabling AI to generate human-like text, translate languages, and even reason through complex problems. However, as impressive as traditional transformers are, they come with inherent inefficiencies—wasting computational power on less important data and demanding massive amounts of hardware to function effectively. Mixture of Depths (MoD) marks a major breakthrough by addressing these inefficiencies, offering key improvements over previous transformer architectures.

One of the most significant enhancements MoD brings is selective computation, which allows the model to focus its processing power only on the most relevant tokens. Unlike traditional transformers that allocate equal resources to every token in a sequence, MoD dynamically adjusts how much computation each token receives. This means that instead of treating every word or symbol as equally important, the model identifies which tokens require deep analysis and which can bypass certain layers without affecting performance. The result is a leaner, faster AI that delivers equal or superior accuracy while consuming far fewer resources.

Another crucial improvement is the reduction in floating point operations per second (FLOPs)—a key metric for measuring computational cost. MoD significantly reduces the number of FLOPs per forward pass, making it possible to train and deploy AI models with far lower hardware requirements. This efficiency not only cuts costs but also enables researchers and businesses to work with larger-scale models without requiring expensive computational infrastructure. In some configurations, MoD models have been shown to outperform traditional transformers despite using fewer FLOPs, proving that intelligent allocation of resources is just as important as raw computational power.

MoD also introduces a static computational framework, which ensures predictable and efficient hardware utilization. Many AI optimizations attempt to reduce computation dynamically, but they often introduce unpredictability, making it harder for hardware to run AI processes efficiently. MoD avoids this issue by setting predefined limits on how many tokens undergo full computation, ensuring a balance between flexibility and stability. This approach allows AI models to remain scalable and efficient without disrupting performance.

One of the most surprising advantages of MoD is that it not only reduces computational overhead but also improves overall performance. Research has shown that by skipping unnecessary calculations, MoD allows AI models to be trained for longer durations or on larger datasets within the same budget, leading to better generalization and higher accuracy. In contrast, traditional transformers often hit limitations where adding more computation leads to diminishing returns. MoD breaks this pattern by making computation more strategic, ensuring that AI models continue improving without excessive resource consumption.

Additionally, MoD is highly compatible with other AI optimizations, including Mixture of Experts (MoE). By integrating MoD with MoE, AI models can not only skip unnecessary computations but also intelligently route information between different processing pathways, further enhancing efficiency. This combination unlocks new possibilities for scalable, high-performance AI systems that can operate at unprecedented levels of efficiency.

In essence, MoD represents a fundamental shift in how AI models are designed. Instead of simply making models bigger and more computationally expensive, it introduces a smarter way of processing information, making AI systems faster, more cost-effective, and more scalable. As AI continues to advance, breakthroughs like MoD will be essential in pushing the boundaries of what's possible, ensuring that AI remains both powerful and practical for real-world applications.

Chapter 3: The Science Behind MoD – Breaking Down the Mechanism

Artificial intelligence has always been about pattern recognition—identifying important signals within vast amounts of data and making sense of them. However, traditional transformer models process every token in a sequence with equal intensity, even when many of those tokens contribute little to the final output. This inefficiency has long been a major challenge in AI, making models expensive to train and operate. Mixture of Depths (MoD) changes this by introducing a more intelligent way to process information, selectively routing only the most relevant data through deep computations while skipping less important details.

At the core of this breakthrough is self-attention, a mechanism that allows AI models to understand the relationships between words or tokens in a given sequence. In traditional transformers, every token undergoes self-attention calculations, which determine how much influence each token should have on others. These calculations are computationally expensive, especially for long sequences, as every token needs to compare itself against all others. MoD optimizes this process by allowing certain tokens to bypass full self-attention layers when they don't contribute meaningfully to the final prediction.

This selective routing is made possible through multi-layer perceptron (MLP) layers, which act as secondary decision-makers within the model. Instead of treating every token the same way, MoD first passes them through a routing system that assigns each token a score based on its importance. This scoring system is known as Top-K selection, where only the highest-ranked tokens—those most critical to the final output—are given full computational attention. The rest take a shortcut route, avoiding deep self-attention and MLP layers to reduce unnecessary processing.

To visualize this, imagine a group discussion where only a few people contribute meaningful insights, while others simply repeat what has already been said. In a traditional transformer, every participant would be given equal speaking time, leading to redundancy. MoD, on the other hand, acts as a smart moderator, identifying the most insightful speakers (high-scoring tokens) and giving them the floor while letting others remain in the background. This ensures that the key points are processed thoroughly without wasting time on irrelevant chatter.

The Top-K selection process is particularly impactful in long-form text processing, where many words are connectors rather than core ideas. By allowing only the top K tokens to pass through full computation, MoD cuts down on redundant processing, making AI models significantly faster without losing their ability to understand context. The value of K (which determines how many tokens receive full computation) is preset, ensuring that hardware utilization remains predictable and efficient. This allows MoD to operate within a static computation graph, avoiding the unpredictability that often comes with dynamic AI optimizations.

The impact of this innovation is profound. With MoD, AI models can scale larger, process information faster, and operate with significantly lower computational costs. This not only makes AI more accessible for researchers and businesses but also opens the door for real-time applications where speed and efficiency are critical. Whether it's enhancing language models, improving search engines, or optimizing real-time AI assistants, MoD's selective routing strategy is a game-changer, ensuring that AI models are not just powerful but also intelligent in how they use their resources.

Artificial intelligence, particularly in large-scale language models, relies on the ability to process vast amounts of data efficiently while maintaining accuracy. One of the most important mechanisms that help achieve this balance is the use of residual connections. These connections play a crucial role in Mixture of Depths (MoD), ensuring that even when certain tokens bypass full computation, the model still retains a flow of information that prevents degradation in performance.

Residual connections act as a shortcut path that allows information to pass through the model without undergoing full transformations at every layer. This means that even when a token is not routed through deep self-attention or MLP layers, it does not entirely lose access to the knowledge being built at different stages of processing. Instead, it maintains a reference to previous computations, ensuring that even lightly processed tokens still contribute to the overall understanding of the input. This is especially critical in MoD's approach because it allows the model to be highly selective without completely discarding potentially valuable information.

Another critical aspect of MoD's efficiency is its reliance on static computation graphs, which help optimize hardware utilization. Many AI models today use dynamic computation graphs, meaning that the pathway of data processing can change depending on input conditions. While this flexibility can sometimes improve adaptability, it comes at the cost of computational unpredictability, leading to inefficient hardware usage, increased latency, and difficulty in parallel processing.

MoD, in contrast, takes a structured approach by setting predefined limits on how many tokens receive full computation. This ensures that hardware operations remain predictable and optimized, allowing AI accelerators like GPUs and TPUs to process data more efficiently. By maintaining a fixed computational structure, MoD eliminates the overhead that typically arises from managing variable-length processing paths. This structured design makes it possible to allocate resources more effectively, keeping power consumption lower and enabling larger-scale training on the same budget.

However, the challenge in AI optimization has always been striking a balance between reducing computational load and maintaining accuracy. Simply skipping computations on certain tokens could risk degrading the model's performance, causing it to lose important context or make inaccurate predictions. MoD overcomes this challenge by integrating per-token routing with controlled sparsity—meaning that the model does not randomly drop computations but rather intelligently selects which parts of the data require deep processing.

Moreover, by interleaving full-capacity layers at regular intervals, MoD ensures that even tokens that were previously skipped get periodically processed with full computational depth. This prevents information loss and allows the model to correct any potential errors that may arise from early-stage filtering. Research has shown that this method not only preserves accuracy but can even improve overall model performance, as it reduces noise from unnecessary computations and allows the AI to focus on what truly matters.

By strategically combining residual connections, static computation graphs, and controlled token selection, MoD achieves a breakthrough in AI efficiency. It is not just about reducing computational costs—it's about rethinking how AI models distribute their intelligence, ensuring they remain both powerful and scalable in the years to come.

Chapter 4: MoD's Impact on AI Performance and Efficiency

Artificial intelligence has long followed a pattern where increased performance is tied to increasing computational power. Traditional transformers have grown exponentially in size, requiring massive processing capabilities to achieve state-of-the-art results. However, Mixture of Depths (MoD) challenges this trend by proving that efficiency, not just raw power, is the key to AI advancement. It introduces a smarter way of processing information—one that allows AI models to achieve equal or superior performance compared to traditional transformers while using significantly fewer computational resources.

At the heart of MoD's advantage is its dynamic processing mechanism, which ensures that only the most relevant tokens receive full computational depth. Traditional transformers waste a vast amount of resources by treating every token equally, even when many contribute little to the final output. MoD solves this inefficiency through intelligent token routing, allowing the model to focus on critical data points while bypassing unnecessary computations. This approach leads to a remarkable efficiency gain, as the model no longer spends resources processing irrelevant tokens.

One of the most striking outcomes of this optimization is that MoD often surpasses traditional transformers in performance metrics despite using fewer FLOPs (floating point operations per second). Researchers found that MoD achieves lower perplexity scores—a key measure of language model accuracy—while requiring fewer computational steps per forward pass. This means that MoD not only reduces processing time but also produces higher-quality results, making it more effective even with limited resources.

A key reason for this performance boost is that MoD avoids over-processing tokens that do not need deep attention, thereby reducing model noise.

In traditional transformers, every token goes through multiple layers of computation, even if it does not significantly influence the model's final decision. This can lead to unnecessary complexity, where the model must filter through irrelevant information before arriving at a conclusion. MoD streamlines this process, ensuring that only meaningful tokens undergo full processing while others take an optimized path. The result is a clearer, more focused AI output, reducing the chance of errors while improving model interpretability.

Beyond accuracy improvements, MoD's efficiency gains translate into practical benefits across industries. AI models that previously required enormous cloud-based infrastructure to function can now be deployed on smaller, more cost-effective hardware, making advanced AI more accessible to businesses and researchers. Training AI models also becomes faster and more scalable, as MoD enables larger networks to be trained within the same computational budget, pushing AI capabilities forward without an exponential increase in cost.

In essence, MoD redefines how AI efficiency is measured. Rather than simply increasing parameter counts and computation, it optimizes resource allocation, ensuring that power is used where it matters most. This not only makes AI models more practical but also sets a new standard for future innovations—one where intelligence is not just about scale but about how effectively AI can learn, adapt, and generate insights with minimal waste.

Artificial intelligence has always faced a tradeoff between power and efficiency. As models grow in complexity, they require more computational resources, more memory, and more time to process information. This has made scaling a challenge—while larger models offer better performance, they often come with astronomical costs in terms of processing power and storage requirements. Mixture of Depths (MoD) fundamentally changes this equation by proving that AI models can scale larger without an exponential increase in cost.

MoD's ability to prioritize critical computations means that instead of blindly applying processing power to every token, the model allocates resources more intelligently. This strategic allocation allows larger models to be trained without consuming significantly more compute power, making it possible to push AI capabilities further while staying within existing computational budgets. In contrast, traditional transformers scale by increasing the number of layers or parameters, which quickly leads to diminishing returns—each additional layer requires exponentially more FLOPs (floating-point operations per second) while providing only marginal performance improvements. MoD bypasses this inefficiency by allowing targeted scaling, ensuring that additional parameters enhance meaningful computations rather than wasting resources on unnecessary calculations.

Beyond enabling larger models, MoD also provides a drastically reduced memory footprint, which directly translates into faster inference speeds. Traditional AI models store a vast amount of intermediate computations, requiring massive memory allocation even for relatively simple tasks. MoD, on the other hand, skips unnecessary layers, reducing the number of intermediate activations that need to be stored and retrieved. This leads to lighter, faster AI models that can process data in real-time without the bottlenecks typically seen in large-scale transformers. In practical applications, this means chatbots that respond instantaneously, AI-powered video editing tools that generate frames without lag, and recommendation systems that deliver personalized results with near-zero delay.

MoD's advantages become even clearer when compared to other transformer optimizations. Many approaches have attempted to reduce AI's computational burden, but they often introduce drawbacks that limit their effectiveness. Sparse transformers, for example, reduce complexity by computing only selective attention scores rather than full attention maps. While this improves efficiency, it introduces a tradeoff in accuracy, as the model must work with incomplete attention information. Mixture of Experts (MoE), another popular optimization, routes different data points to specialized neural network "experts." This method improves efficiency but requires complex coordination between multiple sub-networks, which can introduce communication overhead and unpredictability in hardware performance.

MoD stands out because it achieves efficiency without sacrificing performance. Unlike sparse transformers, it does not discard valuable attention information, and unlike MoE, it maintains a structured, predictable computation graph, making it easier to deploy on existing AI hardware. This predictability in resource allocation makes MoD ideal for applications where both scalability and real-time processing are critical—such as AI-driven medical diagnosis, financial modeling, and large-scale language generation.

Ultimately, MoD is not just another efficiency tweak—it is a fundamental rethinking of how AI should process information. By enabling larger models to be trained without additional cost, reducing memory requirements, and outperforming other optimization methods, MoD is paving the way for the next generation of AI systems—ones that are smarter, faster, and far more scalable than ever before.

Chapter 5: Combining MoD with Mixture of Experts (MoE)

Artificial intelligence has long faced a critical challenge: how to balance powerful processing with efficiency. As models grow larger to improve performance, they become increasingly resource-intensive, demanding enormous amounts of computation, memory, and energy. While Mixture of Depths (MoD) optimizes computation by selectively processing important tokens, another groundbreaking approach—Mixture of Experts (MoE)—further enhances this efficiency by distributing computational tasks among specialized "expert" networks. When combined, MoD and MoE form a hybrid AI architecture that optimally routes information while eliminating unnecessary computations, making AI models significantly more scalable and cost-effective.

Understanding Mixture of Experts (MoE)

MoE is an adaptive AI architecture designed to divide complex tasks among multiple specialized neural networks, or "experts." Instead of using a single, massive network to process all data, MoE creates separate expert sub-networks, each trained to handle specific types of inputs. A gating mechanism then determines which expert (or experts) should process a given token, ensuring that only the most relevant computations are performed. This means that rather than activating the entire model for every input, MoE activates only a fraction of its total parameters per computation, allowing AI to scale efficiently without excessive computational costs.

MoE is particularly effective in large-scale language models, where different types of sentences, words, or structures benefit from specialized processing. For example, in an AI model trained for multilingual translation, certain experts might specialize in grammatical structures, while others might focus on cultural context, sentence formality, or numerical data. The gating mechanism dynamically routes each input to the most relevant experts, ensuring that computations are performed only where needed.

How MoE Enhances MoD

While MoD reduces computational waste by skipping unnecessary processing for less important tokens, MoE takes this a step further by ensuring that even the processed tokens receive only the most specialized attention. This combination creates a highly efficient hybrid system where:

1. MoD filters the input sequence by determining which tokens require full processing and which can skip deep computation. This reduces the number of FLOPs needed per forward pass.
2. MoE further optimizes the computation by dynamically assigning the remaining processed tokens to specialized experts, ensuring that even deep computations are handled efficiently.

3. Both approaches work together to prevent wasted resources, significantly reducing model size, training costs, and inference time while preserving (or even improving) accuracy.

The Hybrid Approach: Smarter Routing, Faster AI

The combination of MoD and MoE introduces a multi-layered optimization strategy:

- Skipping Unnecessary Computations – MoD ensures that redundant tokens don't waste processing power by bypassing deep transformer layers when they are not essential.
- Expert-Level Processing for Key Tokens – MoE ensures that the tokens that do undergo deep processing are routed to the most relevant expert sub-network, reducing inefficiencies.
- Lower Memory Footprint & Faster Inference – Because both MoD and MoE selectively process only the most crucial data, AI models require significantly less memory and compute power

while still maintaining state-of-the-art performance.

Why This Matters for the Future of AI

Traditionally, the only way to improve AI accuracy was to scale models bigger and bigger, leading to massive costs and computational bottlenecks. The MoD + MoE hybrid approach breaks this pattern by demonstrating that AI does not have to process everything equally—it can learn to prioritize, route, and optimize computations intelligently. This shift is crucial as AI applications expand into areas requiring real-time decision-making, on-device processing, and large-scale deployments.

By combining MoD's token-level filtering with MoE's expert-level specialization, Google has created a system that is both smarter and faster, delivering high-quality AI performance without the wasteful resource consumption of traditional transformer models. This marks a major step toward making AI more scalable, cost-effective, and accessible, paving the way for next-generation machine learning architectures that can power everything from advanced language models to real-time AI applications.

Artificial intelligence has long been associated with the idea that bigger is better. The conventional approach to improving AI performance has been to scale models up, increasing the number of parameters, layers, and computational power in an attempt to make them more accurate and capable. This strategy has led to remarkable advances, but it has also introduced a growing problem—diminishing returns. Larger models require exponentially more resources, making them expensive to train and difficult to deploy in real-world applications. The combination of Mixture of Depths (MoD) and Mixture of Experts (MoE) challenges this paradigm by proving that AI can be not just bigger, but also significantly more efficient.

Traditional transformer models process every token with equal computational effort, whether it carries critical meaning or is merely a filler word. This results in unnecessary processing, as many tokens contribute little to the final output. MoD changes this by dynamically adjusting computation, ensuring that only the most meaningful tokens receive full processing while others take a more efficient route. By itself, this approach already reduces computational costs while maintaining or even improving performance, but the introduction of MoE takes efficiency to another level.

MoE works by dividing computational tasks among specialized expert networks, ensuring that even the most critical tokens are handled with maximum efficiency. Instead of forcing a single large model to process everything, MoE activates only a fraction of the total network at any given time, directing specific types of inputs to the experts best suited to handle them. This targeted allocation of resources means that models no longer need to run every computation on every input, dramatically reducing processing requirements. When MoD and MoE are combined, the result is a system that routes computations intelligently, skips redundant processes, and maximizes efficiency without compromising accuracy.

The impact of this hybrid approach is immediately clear when compared to traditional transformers. Training times are reduced, inference speeds are significantly faster, and memory usage is optimized, allowing models to scale without an exponential increase in resource demands. MoD alone has been shown to reduce FLOP usage by nearly 50%, while integrating MoE provides additional gains by ensuring that even the processed tokens receive only the most specialized attention. Together, these techniques allow AI systems to handle larger datasets, more complex queries, and real-time interactions with far greater efficiency than before.

The real power of MoD + MoE lies in how it translates into real-world applications. In natural language processing, where models must understand and generate human-like text, this efficiency gain allows for faster response times, lower latency, and reduced operational costs. AI assistants, search engines, and content recommendation systems can now process queries in a fraction of the time, delivering more accurate results without the computational overhead of traditional models. In AI-driven video generation, MoD ensures that only the most important frames receive full processing, while MoE directs different aspects of the scene—such as motion, lighting, or object details—to specialized networks, resulting in higher quality visuals at lower computational cost.

Beyond consumer applications, this hybrid efficiency is revolutionizing scientific research, medical diagnostics, and autonomous systems. AI models used in drug discovery and genetic research can now analyze vast datasets without the need for massive computing clusters, accelerating breakthroughs in ways that were previously impossible. In self-driving technology, where real-time decision-making is critical, MoD ensures that only the most relevant sensor data is fully processed, while MoE directs specific driving conditions—such as detecting pedestrians or navigating bad weather—to specialized expert networks, improving both speed and safety.

The shift from brute-force computation to intelligent resource allocation represents a major turning point in AI development. Instead of continuing down a path of endlessly increasing model sizes and hardware requirements, MoD + MoE demonstrates that smarter, more efficient AI is not only possible but superior in both performance and scalability. As AI continues to evolve, the emphasis will shift away from raw power and toward precision, adaptability, and efficiency, setting a new standard for the future of machine intelligence.

Chapter 6: The Future of AI Video Generation – Google's V2 Model

The ability to generate high-quality videos from simple text descriptions has long been considered a futuristic concept, but with the introduction of Google's V2 AI video generation model, this vision is becoming a reality. AI-generated content has already reshaped industries such as art, music, and writing, and now video is the next frontier. Unlike previous attempts at AI-powered video generation, which often struggled with consistency, motion realism, and frame coherence, V2 brings a level of sophistication that bridges the gap between human creativity and machine automation.

What sets V2 apart is its ability to transform ordinary text-based prompts into visually compelling, realistic videos, making it an invaluable tool for content creators, marketers, educators, and filmmakers. Traditionally, creating high-quality video content required expensive equipment, specialized skills, and countless hours of editing. V2 dramatically reduces this barrier by allowing anyone to generate professional-looking clips simply by describing what they want to see. Whether it's a cinematic landscape, an animated character, or a complex action scene, V2 processes the input and brings it to life with remarkable detail and fluidity.

The magic behind this model lies in its multi-stage generation process, where AI doesn't just produce a single frame and predict the next, but instead constructs entire video sequences with dynamic movement, natural lighting, and realistic physics. The underlying system uses diffusion models, a technique that gradually refines a video's quality over multiple iterations, ensuring smooth transitions and lifelike motion. Unlike older AI models that generated one frame at a time—often resulting in jittery or unrealistic motion—V2 builds cohesive sequences, giving each clip a natural, flowing appearance.

At the heart of V2's success is its ability to understand context and adapt visuals accordingly. When given a text prompt, the model doesn't just match keywords to images; it interprets the scene holistically, considering factors like perspective, depth, camera angles, and object interactions. If a user requests "a sunset over the ocean with waves crashing against the shore," V2 doesn't just generate an image of a beach—it animates the waves rolling in, adjusts the golden hues of the sunset, and incorporates realistic water reflections, making the scene appear as though it were captured by a professional cinematographer.

This level of precision is made possible by large-scale training on diverse datasets, including real-world footage, physics simulations, and artistic compositions. The model continuously learns from these sources, allowing it to predict movement patterns, apply cinematic techniques, and generate naturalistic textures with a level of accuracy never seen before in AI-generated video. It can even adjust to different artistic styles, meaning a user could request a clip in the style of a hand-drawn animation, a hyper-realistic film, or a vintage documentary.

What makes V2 even more revolutionary is its real-time rendering capability. While traditional CGI and video editing software require extensive rendering times, V2 can generate high-quality video within minutes, making it ideal for rapid prototyping, content previews, and instant storytelling. This means filmmakers can visualize scenes before production, marketers can create promotional videos without a full production team, and educators can generate illustrative content on demand.

Google's V2 isn't just a tool—it's a paradigm shift in video creation, one that redefines how stories are told, how brands engage with audiences, and how creativity is unleashed in the digital age. As AI video technology continues to evolve, the line between imagination and reality grows thinner, opening up a world of possibilities that once seemed impossible.

The ability to generate high-quality videos using AI has always seemed like something reserved for the distant future, but Google's V2 AI video generation model is proving otherwise. With its ability to transform simple text prompts into cinematic, realistic, and visually compelling sequences, this technology is set to redefine content creation. However, like any cutting-edge tool, cost plays a crucial role in determining its accessibility and adoption. Google has structured V2's pricing at 50 cents per second of generated video, translating to about $30 per minute or $1,800 per hour of AI-generated footage.

At first glance, this pricing may seem steep, but when compared to the cost of traditional Hollywood-level production, it becomes clear why this technology is so disruptive. High-end film and video production often requires large crews, expensive equipment, visual effects artists, and extensive post-production work, all of which contribute to costs that can skyrocket into the millions. A blockbuster film like *Avengers: Endgame*, for instance, had an estimated production budget of around $32,000 per second of footage, factoring in CGI, set designs, and editing. Even smaller commercial productions for advertising or short films often require tens of thousands of dollars per minute, making high-quality video production inaccessible to many smaller brands and independent creators.

In contrast, V2 offers an alternative where businesses, content creators, and even individual users can produce visually impressive video content at a fraction of the traditional cost. Instead of hiring a team of animators or renting out production studios, a marketer can simply describe the video they need, let AI generate it, and use the result almost instantly. For brands that frequently need promotional content, social media clips, or explainer videos, this model eliminates long production timelines and reduces costs without compromising quality.

The implications for independent filmmakers and digital creators are particularly exciting. Until now, high-quality visual storytelling has been largely restricted to those with significant budgets and access to professional production tools. With AI-driven video generation, smaller creators can now compete at a higher level, producing polished, cinematic sequences without requiring expensive cameras, lighting, or post-production editing software. This democratization of video production means that even an individual with a creative vision but limited resources can bring their ideas to life in ways that were previously impossible.

For businesses, V2 presents a scalable solution to content creation. Brands that need consistent visual content for advertising, e-commerce, or corporate presentations can now generate videos on demand, reducing their dependency on costly video shoots. This is especially relevant in the digital marketing space, where companies must produce high volumes of engaging content to maintain visibility. Instead of spending weeks coordinating a single commercial shoot, a company can use V2 to generate multiple variations of a campaign video in minutes, allowing for rapid A/B testing and targeted audience engagement.

However, while V2's cost model is significantly lower than traditional production, it still raises important questions about accessibility. Independent users and small businesses may find the per-second pricing structure limiting, especially when creating longer content. Unlike OpenAI's Sora model, which is included in a $200 monthly subscription for ChatGPT Pro users, V2 follows a pay-per-use model, meaning costs can quickly add up depending on how much footage is generated. This difference in pricing strategy may determine which creators and businesses opt for Google's solution over competing AI video tools.

Despite these considerations, the sheer efficiency and affordability of AI-generated video compared to traditional methods make it an invaluable tool for the future of media production. Whether for filmmakers looking to prototype scenes, brands needing quick and high-quality visuals, or educators seeking dynamic instructional videos, V2 offers a new era of AI-powered storytelling—one that significantly lowers costs while expanding creative possibilities. As the technology continues to advance and pricing structures evolve, it's only a matter of time before AI-generated video becomes a standard tool in content creation, much like AI-powered text and image generation today.

Chapter 7: AI and Research – Google's Co-Scientist Breakthrough

The intersection of artificial intelligence and scientific research has always been a space filled with both excitement and skepticism. While AI has made breakthroughs in areas like data analysis, pattern recognition, and predictive modeling, the ability to think, reason, and hypothesize like a scientist has remained an elusive goal—until now. Google's AI Co-Scientist System is redefining what it means for machines to contribute to human knowledge, introducing a model that doesn't just analyze data but actively proposes, tests, and refines scientific hypotheses in ways that mirror human researchers.

At its core, the AI Co-Scientist System is built using a multi-agent architecture, where multiple AI components work together to mimic the process of scientific discovery. Instead of a single model generating conclusions, this system consists of specialized AI agents, each assigned a distinct role in hypothesis generation, critique, refinement, and ranking. These agents operate in tandem, challenging and improving each other's ideas to arrive at the most promising scientific conclusions.

The process begins with the Generation Agent, which formulates an initial set of hypotheses based on available data and prior knowledge. This isn't just a random idea generator—it applies principles of logic, probability, and domain-specific knowledge to create testable theories. Once hypotheses are created, they are passed to the Reflection Agent, which acts as a skeptic, evaluating each hypothesis for consistency, plausibility, and logical soundness. If a hypothesis is deemed weak, it is either discarded or modified for further testing.

Next, the Ranking Agent comes into play, comparing competing hypotheses to determine which ones hold the most promise. This is where the system diverges from traditional AI models, which often operate in a binary right-or-wrong framework. Instead, the AI Co-Scientist employs a competitive evaluation system, ranking hypotheses through a process inspired by ELO ratings—the same system used in chess to rank players based on performance. The idea is simple: stronger hypotheses are given higher ratings, while weaker ones are pushed aside. If a lower-ranked hypothesis successfully challenges a higher-ranked one, it gains points, gradually climbing the ranks in credibility.

This ELO-based ranking system is particularly powerful because it allows hypotheses to compete dynamically. Instead of relying on static rules to determine validity, the system continuously refines its knowledge, learning from both successful and failed ideas. This mirrors how human researchers propose, test, and modify theories over time, refining their understanding through constant iteration. The AI isn't just memorizing existing scientific knowledge—it is actively evolving its approach to problem-solving, allowing it to propose genuinely novel ideas that may not have been previously considered.

One of the most astonishing aspects of this system is its ability to uncover scientific insights that even human experts may overlook. In a landmark demonstration, the AI Co-Scientist was able to solve a decade-old mystery in microbiology in just 48 hours—a problem that human researchers had spent years attempting to decipher. The system correctly hypothesized that certain antibiotic-resistant bacteria acquired viral tail-like structures that allowed them to spread resistance genes more efficiently. What made this achievement particularly remarkable was that the correct answer had never been published anywhere, meaning the AI did not retrieve the solution from an existing database. Instead, it constructed the hypothesis independently, based purely on logical inference and analysis.

This breakthrough is a glimpse into the future of AI-powered scientific research. By eliminating human biases, working around the clock without fatigue, and systematically refining its own ideas, the AI Co-Scientist system offers a fundamentally new approach to discovery—one that could accelerate breakthroughs in medicine, physics, and countless other fields. It represents more than just an advanced AI model; it is a step toward creating an autonomous research assistant capable of generating scientific knowledge in real time. As AI continues to integrate into laboratories and research institutions, the boundary between human and machine-driven science may soon become indistinguishable, leading to a world where AI is not just a tool for research but a partner in the very act of discovery itself.

For over a decade, scientists had been struggling to solve a perplexing mystery in microbiology—how certain bacteria rapidly developed antibiotic resistance, making infections harder to treat and posing a serious threat to public health. Despite extensive research and countless experiments, the underlying mechanism remained elusive. Then, in a stunning demonstration of AI's potential in scientific discovery, Google's AI Co-Scientist System unraveled the mystery in just 48 hours, offering an answer that human researchers had been chasing for years.

At the heart of this breakthrough was the AI's ability to autonomously generate, refine, and validate scientific hypotheses at a speed and scale no human team could match. The system was given access to a vast dataset of microbiological studies, but crucially, the correct solution had never been published anywhere—meaning the AI could not simply retrieve an answer from an existing database. Instead, it had to reason through the problem, analyze potential explanations, and rank competing hypotheses based on plausibility and supporting evidence.

Using its multi-agent approach, the AI first generated multiple hypotheses about how bacteria might be gaining their resistance. These ideas were then subjected to a rigorous process of internal critique, with different AI agents acting as skeptics, eliminating weak theories and improving promising ones. Finally, through its ELO-based ranking system, the AI identified the strongest candidate: certain antibiotic-resistant bacteria were acquiring viral tail-like structures, which allowed them to spread resistance genes between different hosts more efficiently.

This discovery was shocking—not just because it provided an answer to a decade-old question, but because it demonstrated that AI could formulate entirely new scientific theories independent of human input. The hypothesis was later confirmed by human researchers, proving that the AI had outperformed years of manual research in a fraction of the time. More importantly, this breakthrough provided a new target for developing treatments against antibiotic-resistant infections, a crucial step in addressing one of the most pressing global health threats.

The implications of this achievement extend far beyond microbiology. If AI can autonomously generate and validate scientific hypotheses, it has the potential to fundamentally change the pace and nature of research itself. Scientific discovery has traditionally been constrained by time, resources, and human cognitive limits—but an AI that never tires, constantly iterates, and refines its own ideas could revolutionize entire fields overnight.

Imagine AI Co-Scientists applied to cancer research, where it could sift through thousands of genetic markers to identify new treatment pathways. In materials science, it could predict the properties of novel compounds, accelerating the discovery of next-generation superconductors or advanced battery technologies. In astronomy, it could analyze cosmic data and propose new models for understanding dark matter or black holes. The possibilities are staggering.

Beyond discovery, AI could also eliminate dead-end experiments before they even begin, preventing researchers from wasting years chasing theories that are unlikely to yield results. This shift would make research not only faster but also more cost-effective, allowing resources to be directed toward the most promising areas.

What the AI Co-Scientist proved with its antibiotic resistance breakthrough was more than just raw computational power—it demonstrated true scientific reasoning, a capacity for logical inference, and the ability to propose new knowledge. If this technology continues to evolve, we may soon live in a world where AI is not just assisting human scientists but actively pioneering discoveries in ways never before imagined. The very nature of research could be transformed, moving from a slow, trial-and-error process to an era of continuous, AI-driven breakthroughs that reshape our understanding of the world in real-time.

Chapter 8: Google's Secret Project – The Next Wave of AI Video Technology

The world of artificial intelligence moves fast, but sometimes, the most exciting developments aren't the ones making headlines—they're the ones hidden beneath the surface, waiting to be uncovered. In the case of Google's secret AI video generator, codenamed "Robin," the clues weren't announced in a flashy press release or a grand demonstration. Instead, they were buried in the depths of Google's own code, quietly hinting at something much bigger on the horizon.

Tech enthusiasts and AI researchers first stumbled upon references to "Robin" while analyzing snippets of code within Google's internal systems. These weren't just random lines of text—they contained direct mentions of "video generation," "progress messages," and "real-time rendering," all tied to a mysterious new AI model. Unlike V2, Google's widely known AI video generator, Robin appeared to be an unreleased, next-generation project, potentially built to take video generation beyond anything currently available.

The most intriguing part of these findings was that Robin seemed to be referenced alongside Gemini, Google's powerful AI model that currently handles text, images, and multimodal tasks. This suggested that Robin might not be a standalone product, but rather a deeper integration within Google's AI ecosystem—perhaps even a feature set for an upcoming version of Gemini. If true, this would mean Google is working toward a unified platform where text, images, and video creation exist within a single AI model, allowing users to generate complex multimedia content seamlessly from one interface.

Another major clue was that Robin's code included mentions of real-time generation, something that existing AI video models have struggled with. Current AI-generated video technology, even at its most advanced stages, often suffers from slow rendering speeds, motion inconsistencies, and artifacts that make the footage appear unnatural. If Robin is truly capable of real-time AI video generation, it could completely change the way content is produced—allowing users to type a prompt and instantly see a high-quality video generated within seconds.

The potential applications of a system like this are staggering. Imagine a filmmaker being able to visualize entire scenes in real-time, instantly generating cinematic-quality footage before ever setting foot on a set. Marketers could create dynamic ad campaigns on demand, adjusting visuals and messaging in real time based on audience responses. Even live AI-generated entertainment could become possible, where animated films, video game cutscenes, or even interactive virtual worlds are created on the fly, responding dynamically to user input.

Perhaps the most fascinating aspect of Robin is the mystery surrounding it. Unlike V2, which Google has openly discussed, Robin remains unannounced, undisclosed, and largely hidden from public view. Whether this is because Google is refining its capabilities before a major reveal, or because it is part of an experimental project not yet meant for release, remains to be seen. However, what is clear is that Google isn't just stopping at AI-generated video—it's pushing toward a future where AI can generate, edit, and refine video content in real-time, with near-human precision.

For now, Robin remains an enigma. But if history is any indicator, when Google quietly develops something behind closed doors, it's usually because they're working on something groundbreaking. And if Robin is indeed the next step in AI-powered video creation, it could mark the beginning of an era where creating high-quality video is as easy as typing a sentence, where ideas instantly materialize into visuals, and where AI-generated storytelling becomes indistinguishable from reality.

The evolution of artificial intelligence has always followed a trajectory toward seamless, multimodal integration—the ability to process and generate different types of content, from text and images to audio and video, within a single system. Google's Gemini AI has already made significant strides in this direction, demonstrating its capability to handle text-based reasoning, image analysis, and multimodal interactions. But the biggest leap is still ahead: the full integration of text, image, and video generation into one unified AI platform.

The clues surrounding Google's unreleased Robin AI video generator, combined with the existing capabilities of Gemini, suggest that Google is quietly building a next-generation multimodal AI system that can generate and manipulate text, images, and video interchangeably. This would represent a complete shift in how AI-powered content creation works, allowing users to move fluidly between different types of media without needing separate tools or platforms.

Imagine a world where you start with a text prompt, generate an image based on it, and then extend that image into a full-motion video—all within a single AI model. A user could type:

"A futuristic city at sunset, flying cars moving through neon-lit skyscrapers"—and not only receive a high-quality image but also have the option to animate it instantly, with AI predicting realistic motion, lighting changes, and dynamic elements. Instead of requiring separate AI models for different tasks, Gemini could act as the core intelligence driving a unified experience.

One of the biggest limitations of current AI video models, including V2 and its competitors, is the fragmented workflow—users must rely on different tools to edit, extend, and refine generated content. If Gemini integrates video alongside text and image capabilities, it could introduce a truly consumer-friendly AI video generation platform, where anyone—from independent creators to marketing professionals—can generate, edit, and enhance videos in real time, without needing advanced editing software.

The potential applications of a fully integrated system like this are enormous. Content creators could generate high-quality animated scenes with just a few words, instantly tweak elements by providing textual feedback, or even modify the style, pacing, or motion dynamics of a video in real time. Businesses could produce personalized marketing videos on demand, adapting footage for different audiences without the need for expensive reshoots or post-production editing. Even industries like education and training could benefit, with AI-generated videos dynamically adapting to the needs of students, creating real-time visual explanations based on text-based queries.

For the everyday consumer, this means that AI-generated video creation could become as common as using a photo filter or typing a chat message. Social media influencers, small businesses, educators, and even casual users could generate polished, professional-grade content without requiring specialized skills or costly production teams. The barriers to entry in video production would shrink dramatically, giving rise to a new era of AI-assisted creativity.

The big question now is not if, but when Google will integrate these capabilities into a single AI-powered ecosystem. Given the increasing competition in AI video generation—especially with OpenAI's Sora model, which has already introduced impressive advancements—Google will likely push to bring its own multimodal AI to market soon. Whether through an advanced version of Gemini or a dedicated consumer-friendly platform, the goal is clear: to make AI-generated video as intuitive, seamless, and powerful as possible.

As AI continues to blur the lines between imagination and reality, the integration of text, image, and video in one unified system will mark a turning point in content creation. The future of AI isn't just about generating individual pieces of media—it's about creating a world where ideas can be instantly transformed into visual stories, effortlessly blending across multiple formats in real time.

Chapter 9: Ethical and Practical Considerations of AI Growth

Artificial intelligence is evolving at a pace that even its creators struggle to keep up with. What started as simple algorithms capable of basic pattern recognition has transformed into models that can generate human-like text, create photorealistic images, and now, even produce high-quality AI-generated videos from text prompts. With each breakthrough, AI becomes more powerful, more autonomous, and more embedded in daily life. While this progress is exciting, it also raises serious concerns about the potential risks associated with AI's rapid development—risks that extend far beyond technical limitations and into the fabric of society itself.

One of the most pressing concerns is bias in AI decision-making. AI systems are trained on vast amounts of data, much of which reflects historical and societal biases. Whether it's a language model generating biased outputs, an AI hiring system favoring certain demographics, or facial recognition disproportionately misidentifying individuals from minority groups, AI inherits the flaws of the data it is trained on. And because these systems operate at scale, their mistakes can reinforce and amplify inequalities at a level never seen before.

Then there's the issue of misinformation. AI-generated content, including realistic deepfake videos and AI-written articles, has made it increasingly difficult to distinguish between what is real and what is artificially constructed. This poses a profound threat to journalism, politics, and public discourse, as malicious actors can use AI to fabricate convincing but false narratives. With AI models like Google's V2 and OpenAI's Sora capable of generating ultra-realistic videos, the possibility of deepfake propaganda, identity fraud, and widespread disinformation campaigns becomes a legitimate concern.

Beyond ethical risks, AI also presents an existential challenge to the workforce. Automation has already disrupted industries, but the next wave of AI advancements threatens not just manual labor but also knowledge-based professions. Jobs that once required human creativity and expertise—such as graphic design, video production, customer service, and even aspects of legal and medical professions—are now being supplemented, if not replaced, by AI. AI-generated videos that took professional teams weeks to create can now be generated in minutes. Writing, translation, and coding can be done in seconds instead of hours. The more AI improves, the harder it becomes to predict which jobs will remain and which will be entirely transformed.

This shift raises difficult questions: Should AI companies be responsible for job displacement? Should governments regulate AI's development to protect workers? How do we ensure that AI's economic benefits are distributed fairly rather than concentrating power in the hands of a few tech giants?

Some argue that AI will create as many jobs as it eliminates, just as past technological revolutions have done. The industrial revolution displaced manual laborers but created entirely new industries. The internet eliminated some jobs while creating countless opportunities in digital marketing, software development, and e-commerce. But the speed of AI's evolution is unlike anything before. The transition between old and new jobs may happen too quickly for the workforce to adapt, leaving millions of people unprepared for an AI-driven economy.

The ethical dilemmas of AI are not just theoretical; they are unfolding in real-time. Regulators are already scrambling to put guardrails in place, from copyright laws protecting artists from AI-generated content to bans on certain AI applications, such as real-time biometric surveillance. However, AI development is often outpacing regulation, meaning that by the time policymakers react, the technology has already evolved to a new level.

The challenge now is not just about advancing AI but about doing so responsibly. Can AI be developed in a way that minimizes harm while maximizing benefits? Can regulations keep up with AI's exponential growth without stifling innovation? And most importantly, how do we ensure that AI serves humanity rather than replacing it?

AI's rapid progress is a double-edged sword—one that holds immense potential but also profound risks. As companies like Google push forward with models that generate text, images, and now high-quality video at an unprecedented level, the world must grapple with the consequences. The choices made today will determine whether AI becomes a tool that uplifts society or one that deepens its inequalities, distorts reality, and reshapes the workforce in unpredictable ways.

As artificial intelligence continues to advance at an astonishing pace, the challenge is no longer just about pushing technological boundaries but about ensuring that these advancements are used responsibly. Google, being one of the most influential players in the AI space, faces immense pressure to balance innovation with ethical considerations, public trust, and regulatory compliance. While AI models like Gemini and V2 AI video generation unlock groundbreaking possibilities, they also introduce risks that require careful management. Google's approach to responsible AI usage involves a combination of internal safeguards, regulatory cooperation, and self-imposed ethical frameworks aimed at preventing misuse while still fostering innovation.

One of Google's primary strategies for ensuring ethical AI deployment is bias mitigation. AI systems, particularly those trained on massive datasets, often reflect the biases present in their training data. Whether in language models, hiring algorithms, or facial recognition systems, biased outputs can have real-world consequences, disproportionately affecting marginalized communities. To counteract this, Google incorporates diverse datasets, fairness algorithms, and human oversight into its AI development pipeline. By continuously refining how AI learns from data, Google aims to reduce unintended bias and promote more equitable decision-making across its AI products.

Another critical aspect of responsible AI usage is misuse prevention, particularly in areas like deepfake detection and AI-generated misinformation. With tools like V2 capable of producing highly realistic AI-generated videos, the potential for fraud, political manipulation, and disinformation campaigns becomes a legitimate concern. Google is actively researching ways to integrate watermarking, provenance tracking, and AI-detection systems to differentiate authentic content from AI-generated material. These efforts are meant to ensure that AI remains a tool for creativity and innovation rather than deception and manipulation.

Google has also embraced AI ethics guidelines that focus on transparency, accountability, and safety. This means AI decisions should be explainable, allowing users to understand how and why certain outputs are generated. In critical areas like healthcare AI and financial models, where AI-driven decisions can impact people's lives, Google works to ensure that models are interpretable rather than black-box systems that operate without clear reasoning.

However, ensuring responsible AI usage is not just an internal challenge—it is also a regulatory battle. Governments and international bodies are increasingly scrutinizing AI companies, demanding clearer rules around data privacy, model transparency, and ethical boundaries. The European Union's AI Act, for example, seeks to impose strict guidelines on high-risk AI applications, while the U.S. and other nations are considering regulations on AI-generated content, privacy protections, and workforce displacement.

Google has positioned itself as a collaborator rather than a disruptor in regulatory discussions, actively engaging with policymakers to shape AI laws that balance safety and innovation.

The difficulty, however, is that regulation often lags behind innovation. AI evolves at exponential speeds, meaning by the time a law is drafted and passed, the technology has already advanced to a new level. If regulations are too rigid, they risk stifling AI development and preventing breakthroughs that could benefit society. If they are too loose, they could allow unchecked AI advancements to spiral out of control, leading to ethical and security risks. Google, like many other AI companies, is walking a fine line—advocating for responsible regulation while ensuring that AI research remains unrestricted enough to drive progress.

One of the biggest unresolved questions is who holds responsibility when AI makes mistakes? If an AI-generated video spreads false information or an

AI-driven hiring system discriminates against certain applicants, should the blame fall on the company, the user, or the AI itself? These dilemmas are why the debate between self-regulation versus government-imposed rules continues to intensify. While Google is investing in internal safeguards, transparency, and ethical AI initiatives, public and legal scrutiny will only increase as AI becomes more deeply integrated into daily life.

The challenge ahead is not just about building smarter AI but about ensuring it serves society without creating unintended harm. Striking a balance between innovation and regulation is crucial—too much control, and AI's potential is limited; too little, and its risks could outweigh its benefits. Google's role in shaping this balance will be one of the defining factors in the future of AI—whether as a force for progress or a technology that requires constant vigilance to prevent unintended consequences.

Conclusion

Artificial intelligence is no longer just a tool for automation; it has evolved into a force that is reshaping how we create, learn, and innovate. The breakthroughs discussed throughout this book—Mixture of Depths (MoD), V2 AI video generation, and the AI Co-Scientist system—represent a new era where AI is not just performing tasks but thinking, adapting, and even discovering in ways that were once the sole domain of humans.

MoD has proven that AI models don't need to grow endlessly in size to improve performance. Instead of the traditional brute-force approach of processing every token with equal effort, MoD introduces a smarter way of computing—allocating resources dynamically, skipping unnecessary computations, and focusing only on what truly matters. This breakthrough alone is revolutionizing how AI models are designed, making them more scalable, efficient, and accessible to industries that once found them too costly or impractical to deploy.

Meanwhile, V2 AI video generation has unlocked an entirely new form of digital storytelling. What once required teams of artists, editors, and expensive production equipment can now be achieved with a simple text prompt. The implications for filmmakers, marketers, educators, and digital content creators are enormous. While AI-generated video won't replace human creativity, it will serve as a powerful tool to accelerate production, lower costs, and democratize high-quality video creation. As AI video models continue to improve, we are approaching a future where the barriers to professional-level content creation are virtually eliminated.

Perhaps the most mind-blowing development is Google's AI Co-Scientist system, which shattered expectations by solving a decade-old microbiology mystery in just 48 hours. This isn't just AI summarizing research—it's forming original scientific hypotheses, testing them, refining them, and arriving at conclusions faster than any human researcher ever could. The implications of this technology stretch far beyond a single discovery; it signals a future where AI could revolutionize drug discovery, physics, space exploration, and nearly every field of scientific inquiry. Instead of waiting years for breakthroughs, AI-powered research assistants could accelerate the pace of discovery exponentially, tackling problems that were once thought to be unsolvable.

These advancements aren't just changing specific industries; they are redefining human capabilities altogether. AI is shifting from being a passive tool to an active collaborator, capable of enhancing creativity, refining knowledge, and even pushing the boundaries of what we understand about the world. But this rapid evolution also comes with challenges—issues of bias, misinformation, ethical responsibility, and economic impact will need to be carefully managed to ensure AI is developed responsibly.

As we stand at the intersection of human intelligence and machine intelligence, the choices made today will determine whether AI becomes a force for progress or a disruptive force with unforeseen consequences. What is certain, however, is that there is no turning back. The world is entering an AI-driven future, and the advancements discussed in this book—MoD's efficiency, V2's creative power, and the Co-Scientist's groundbreaking reasoning abilities—are only the beginning.

In the years ahead, AI will redefine industries, accelerate innovation, and challenge our very understanding of what is possible. Whether it is in the hands of artists, researchers, engineers, or everyday users, AI is set to become the most transformative force of our generation. The future isn't just about machines becoming more intelligent—it's about how we, as a society, choose to harness this intelligence to shape the world we want to live in.

www.ingramcontent.com/pod-product-compliance
Lightning Source LLC
LaVergne TN
LVHW051715050326

832903LV00032B/4206